PERCUSSION
BROADWAY FAVORITES

Solos and Band Arrangements
Correlated with Essential Elements Band Method

Arranged by
MICHAEL SWEENEY

Welcome to Essential Elements Broadway Favorites! This Percussion book includes parts for both Percussion 1 and Percussion 2 of the full band arrangements. A SOLO version of these selections may be found in the Keyboard Percussion book. The supplemental CD recording or PIANO ACCOMPANIMENT BOOK may be used as an accompaniment for solo performance. Use these recordings when playing solos for friends and family.

ISBN 978-0-7935-9856-4

HAL•LEONARD®
CORPORATION
7777 W. BLUEMOUND RD. P.O. BOX 13819 MILWAUKEE, WI 53213

00860050

From Walt Disney's BEAUTY AND THE BEAST: THE BROADWAY MUSICAL

BEAUTY AND THE BEAST

PERCUSSION 1
Sus. Cym., S.D., B.D.

Lyrics by HOWARD ASHMAN
Music by ALAN MENKEN
Arranged by MICHAEL SWEENEY

BEAUTY AND THE BEAST

PERCUSSION 2
Sus. Cym., Claves, Tamb., Tri.

Lyrics by HOWARD ASHMAN
Music by ALAN MENKEN
Arranged by MICHAEL SWEENEY

From the Musical Production ANNIE
TOMORROW

PERCUSSION 1
Hi-Hat, S.D., B.D., Sus. Cym.

Lyric by MARTIN CHARNIN
Music by CHARLES STROUSE
Arranged by MICHAEL SWEENEY

TOMORROW

PERCUSSION 2
Shaker, Triangle, Tambourine

Lyric by MARTIN CHARNIN
Music by CHARLES STROUSE
Arranged by MICHAEL SWEENEY

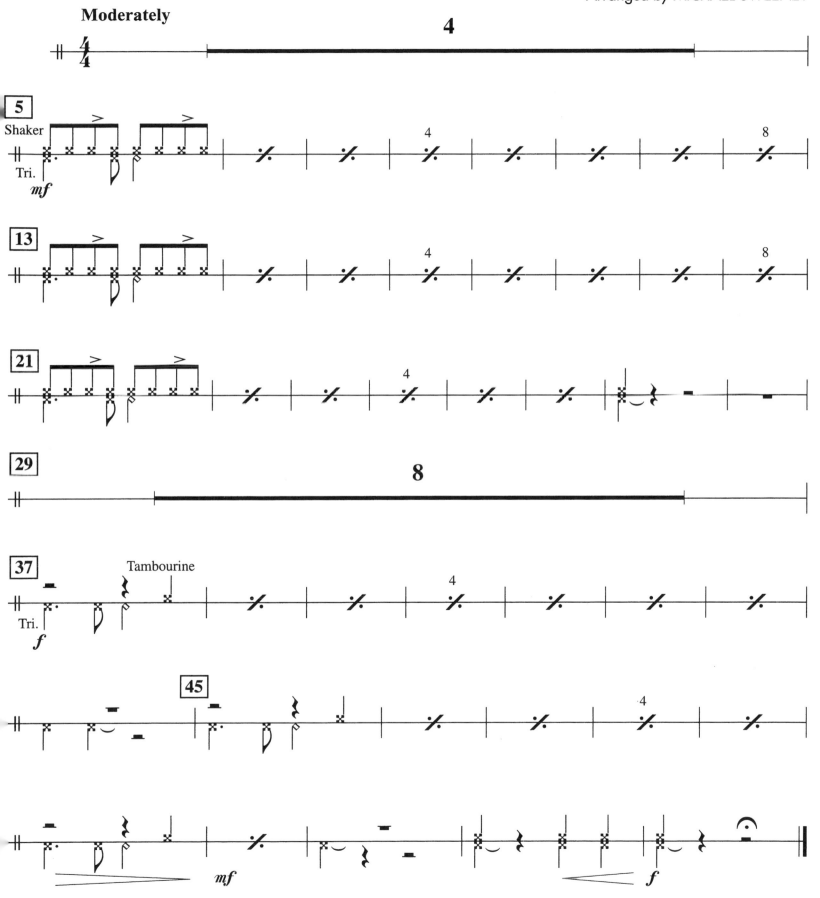

From the Musical CABARET

CABARET

PERCUSSION 1
Snare Drum, Bass Drum

Words by FRED EBB
Music by JOHN KANDER
Arranged by MICHAEL SWEENEY

CABARET

Words by FRED EBB
Music by JOHN KANDER
Arranged by MICHAEL SWEENEY

PERCUSSION 2
Cr. Cym.

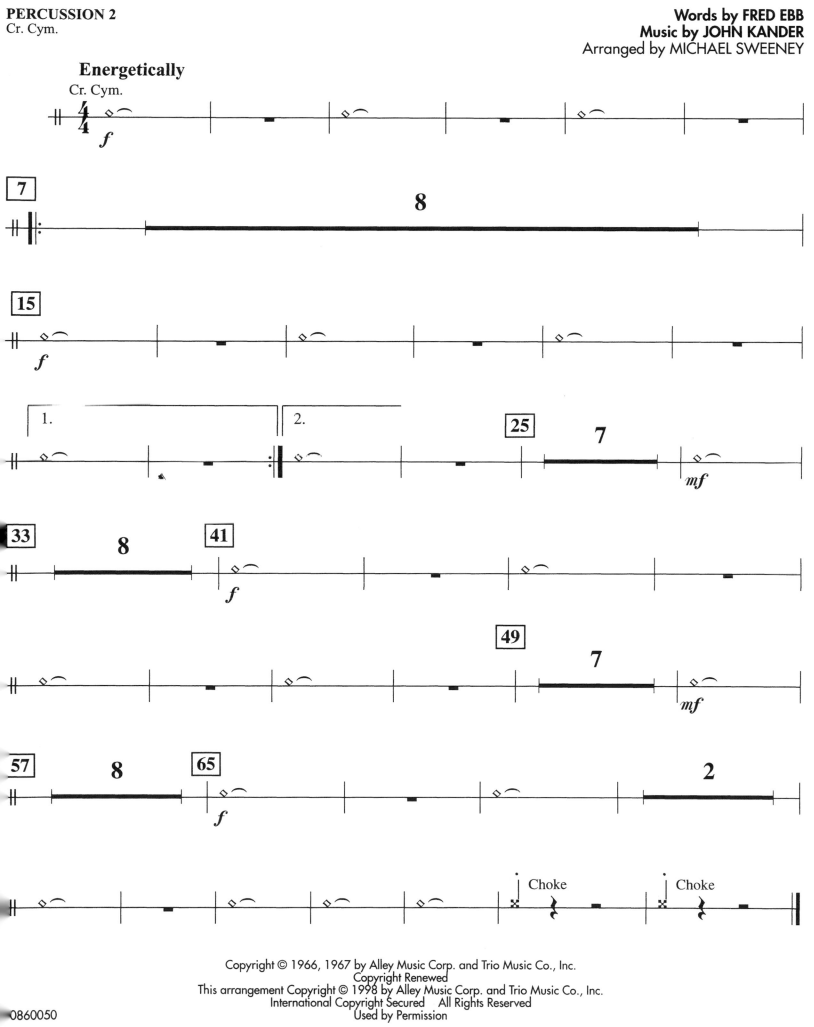

From THE SOUND OF MUSIC
EDELWEISS

PERCUSSION 1
Snare Drum, Bass Drum, Sus. Cym.

Lyrics by OSCAR HAMMERSTEIN II
Music by RICHARD RODGERS
Arranged by MICHAEL SWEENEY

From THE SOUND OF MUSIC
EDELWEISS

PERCUSSION 2
Sus. Cym., Triangle

Lyrics by OSCAR HAMMERSTEIN II
Music by RICHARD RODGERS
Arranged by MICHAEL SWEENEY

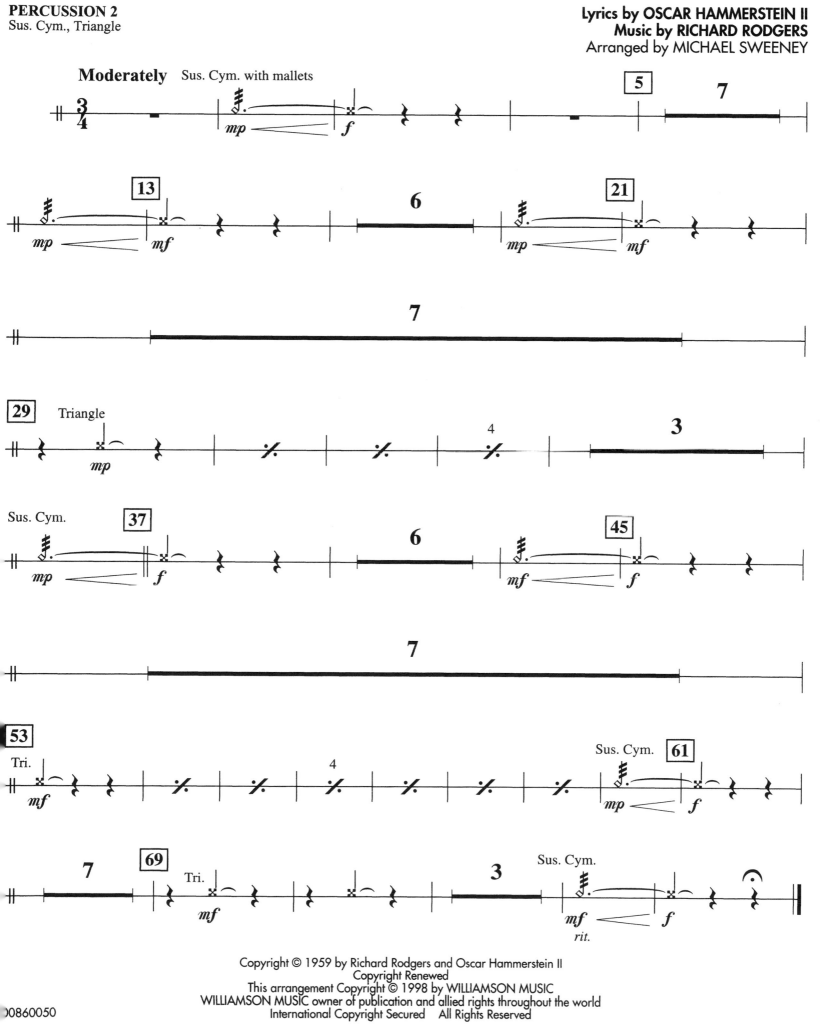

From EVITA
DON'T CRY FOR ME ARGENTINA

Words by TIM RICE
Music by ANDREW LLOYD WEBBER
Arranged by MICHAEL SWEENEY

PERCUSSION 1
Snare Drum, Bass Drum, Sus. Cym.

MCA Music Publishing

Don't Cry for Me Argentina

PERCUSSION 2
Shaker, Claves, Sus. Cym.

Words by TIM RICE
Music by ANDREW LLOYD WEBBER
Arranged by MICHAEL SWEENEY

GET ME TO THE CHURCH ON TIME

Words by ALAN JAY LERNER
Music by FREDERICK LOEWE
Arranged by MICHAEL SWEENEY

PERCUSSION 1
Snare Drum, Bass Drum

GET ME TO THE CHURCH ON TIME

PERCUSSION 2
Cr. Cym.

Words by ALAN JAY LERNER
Music by FREDERICK LOEWE
Arranged by MICHAEL SWEENEY

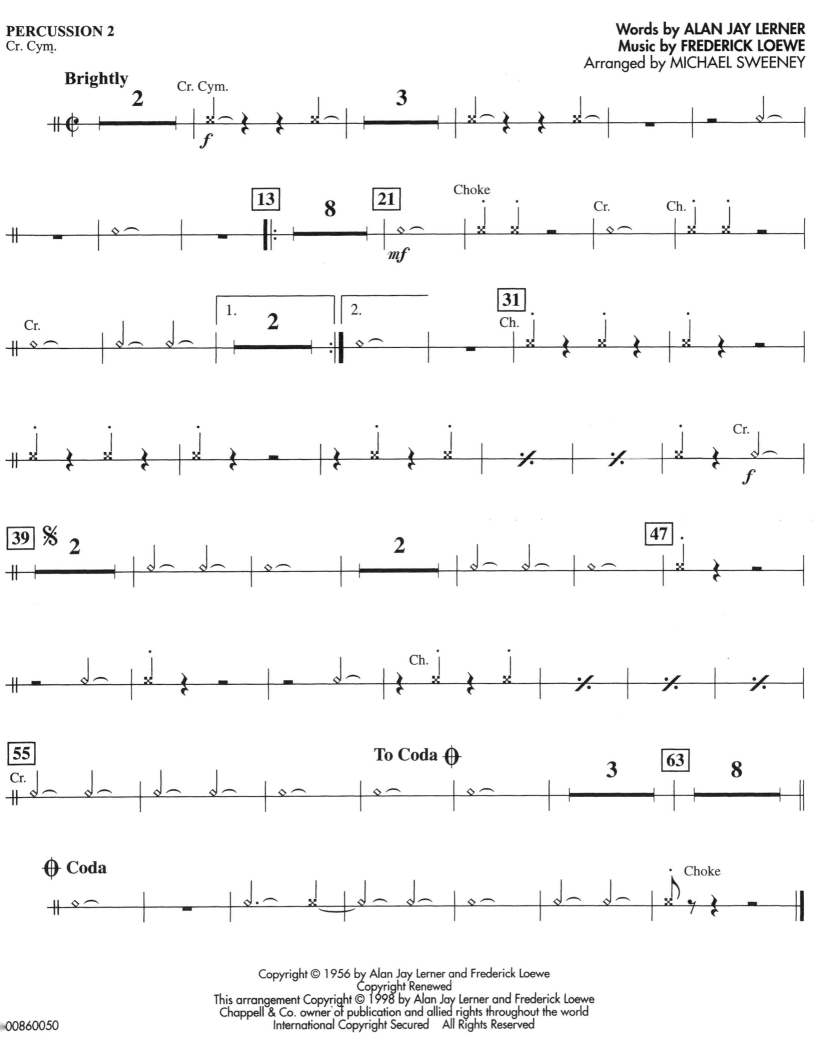

00860050

From LES MISÉRABLES

I DREAMED A DREAM

PERCUSSION 1
Sus. Cym., S.D., B.D.

Music by CLAUDE-MICHEL SCHÖNBERG
Lyrics by ALAIN BOUBLIL,
JEAN-MARC NATEL and HERBERT KRETZMER
Arranged by MICHAEL SWEENEY

From LES MISÉRABLES
I DREAMED A DREAM

PERCUSSION 2
Sus. Cym., Wind Chimes

Music by CLAUDE-MICHEL SCHÖNBERG
Lyrics by ALAIN BOUBLIL,
JEAN-MARC NATEL and HERBERT KRETZMER
Arranged by MICHAEL SWEENEY

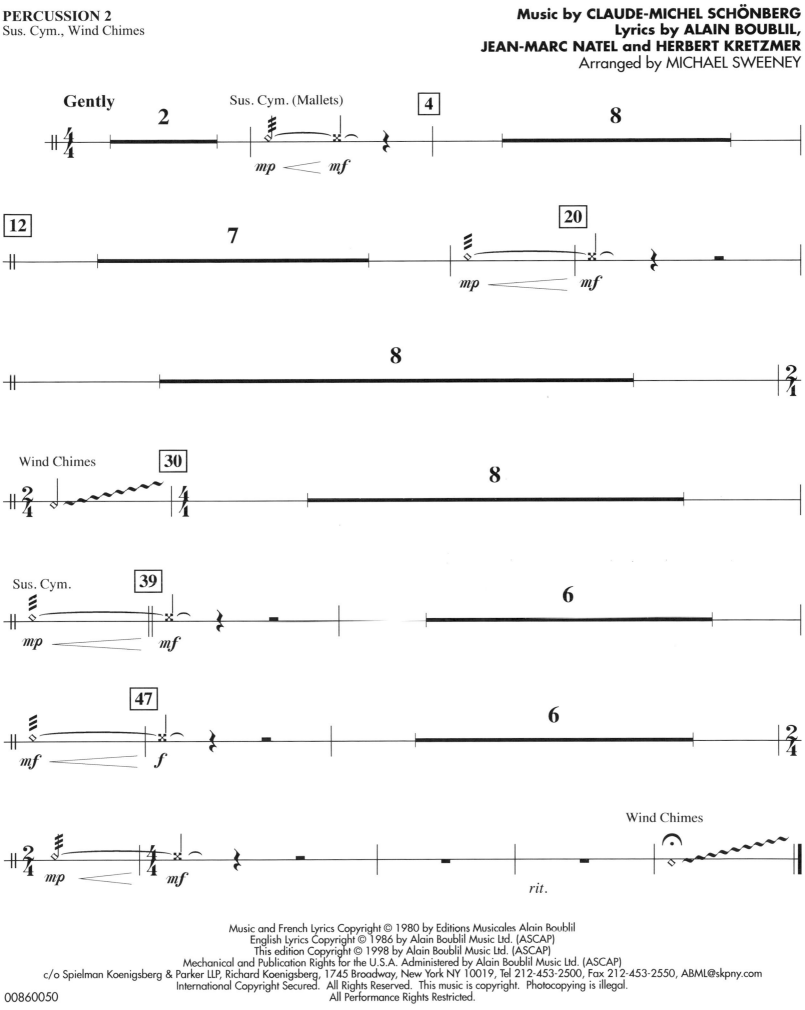

00860050

GO GO GO JOSEPH

PERCUSSION 1
Sus. Cym., S.D., B.D., Hi-Hat

Music by **ANDREW LLOYD WEBBER**
Lyrics by **TIM RICE**
Arranged by **MICHAEL SWEENEY**

GO, GO, GO JOSEPH

PERCUSSION 2
Sus. Cym., Tamb., Bongos, Cr. Cym.

Music by ANDREW LLOYD WEBBER
Lyrics by TIM RICE
Arranged by MICHAEL SWEENEY

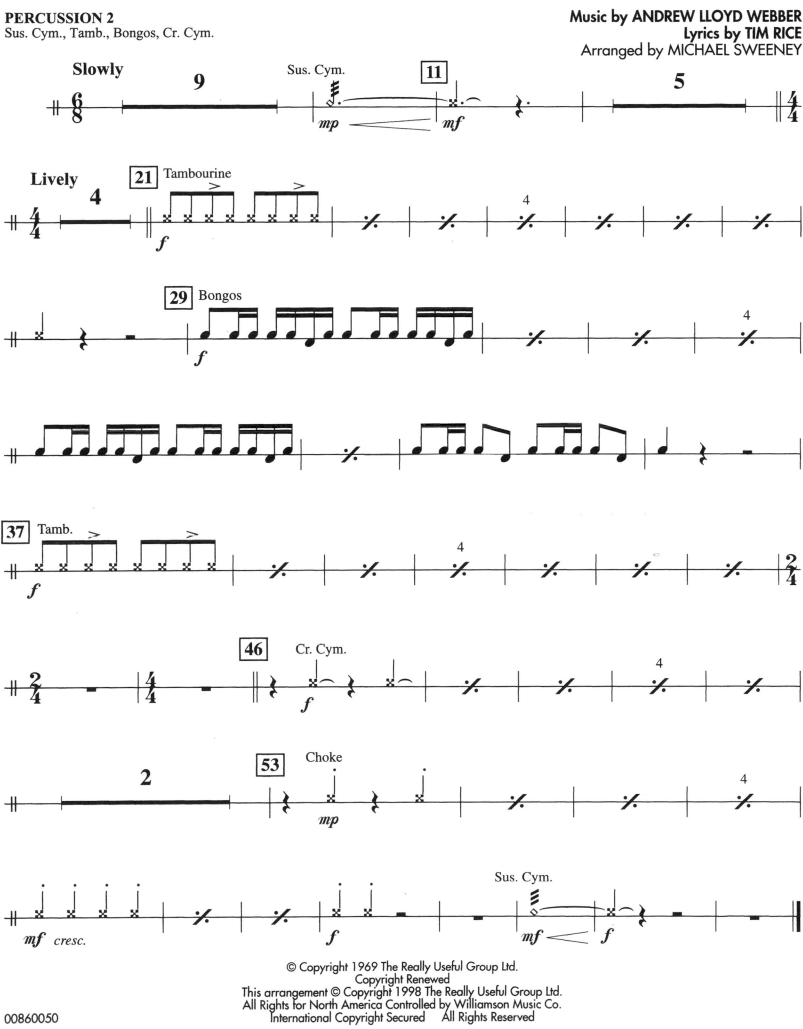

From CATS
MEMORY

PERCUSSION 1
S.D., B.D., Sus. Cym.

Music by ANDREW LLOYD WEBBER
Text by TREVOR NUNN after T.S. ELIOT
Arranged by MICHAEL SWEENEY

From CATS
MEMORY

PERCUSSION 2
Sus. Cym., Tri., Mark Tree

Music by ANDREW LLOYD WEBBER
Text by TREVOR NUNN after T.S. ELIOT
Arranged by MICHAEL SWEENEY

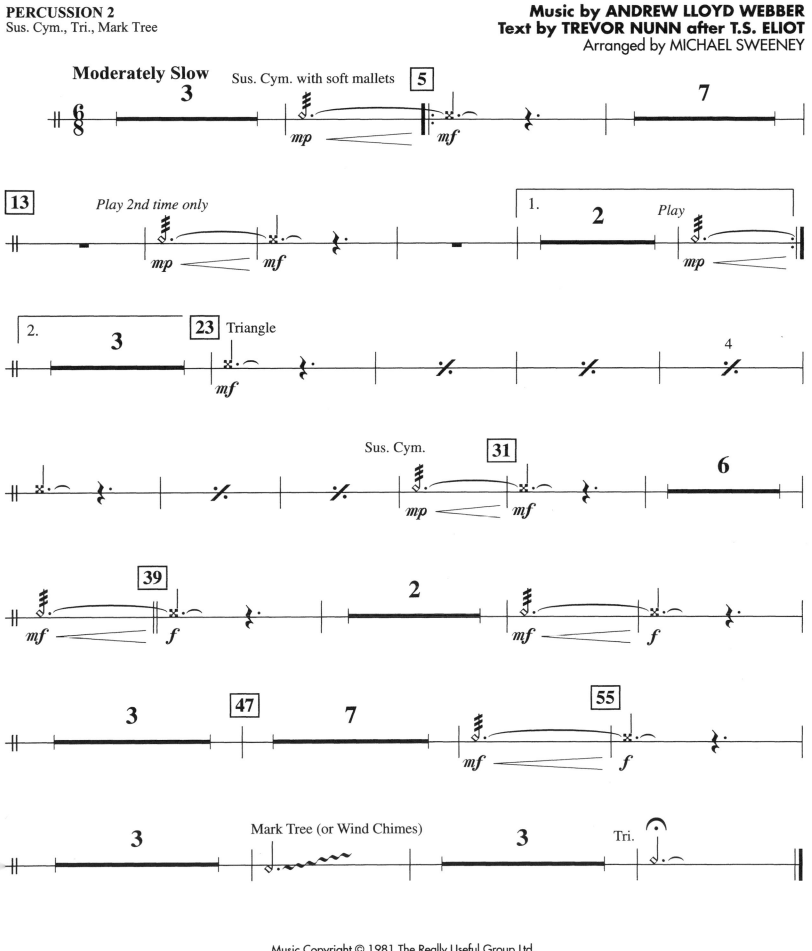

From THE PHANTOM OF THE OPERA

THE PHANTOM OF THE OPERA

PERCUSSION 1
Snare Drum, Bass Drum

Music by ANDREW LLOYD WEBBER
Lyrics by CHARLES HART
Additional Lyrics by RICHARD STILGOE and MIKE BATT
Arranged by MICHAEL SWEENEY

THE PHANTOM OF THE OPERA

PERCUSSION 2
Cr. Cym., Sus. Cym., Tri.

Music by ANDREW LLOYD WEBBER
Lyrics by CHARLES HART
Additional Lyrics by RICHARD STILGOE and MIKE BATT
Arranged by MICHAEL SWEENEY

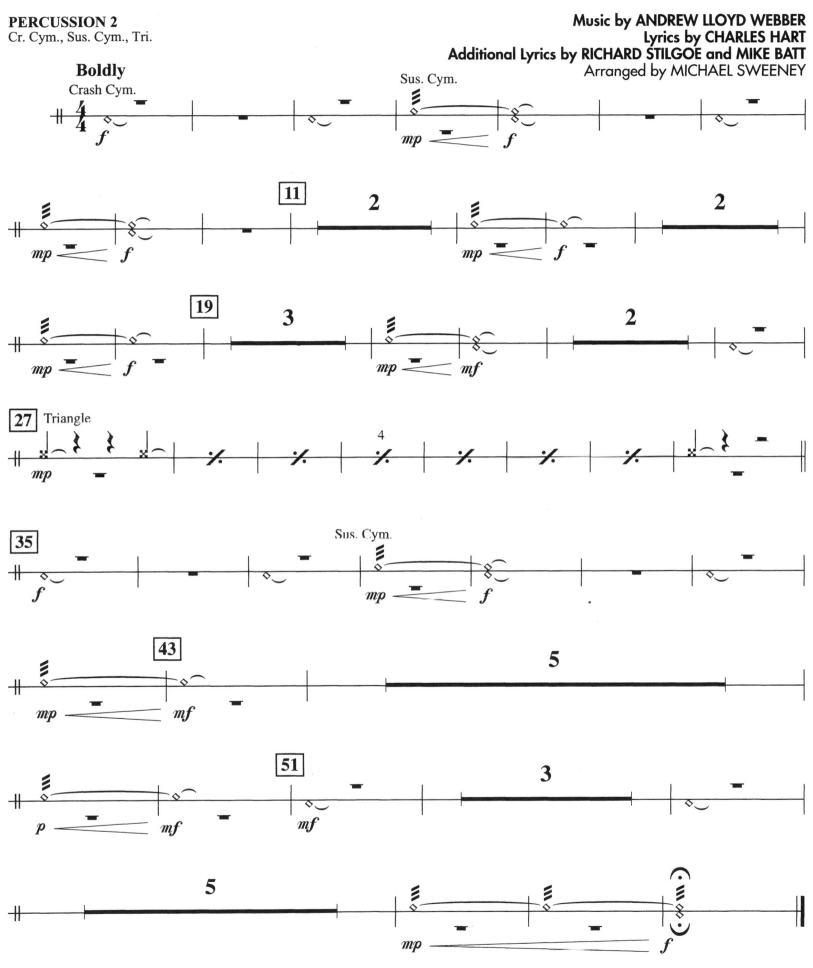

00860050

From Meredith Willson's THE MUSIC MAN

SEVENTY-SIX TROMBONES

PERCUSSION 1
Snare Drum, Bass Drum

By MEREDITH WILLSON
Arranged by MICHAEL SWEENEY

SEVENTY-SIX TROMBONES

PERCUSSION 2
Cr. Cym., Triangle

By MEREDITH WILLSON
Arranged by MICHAEL SWEENEY

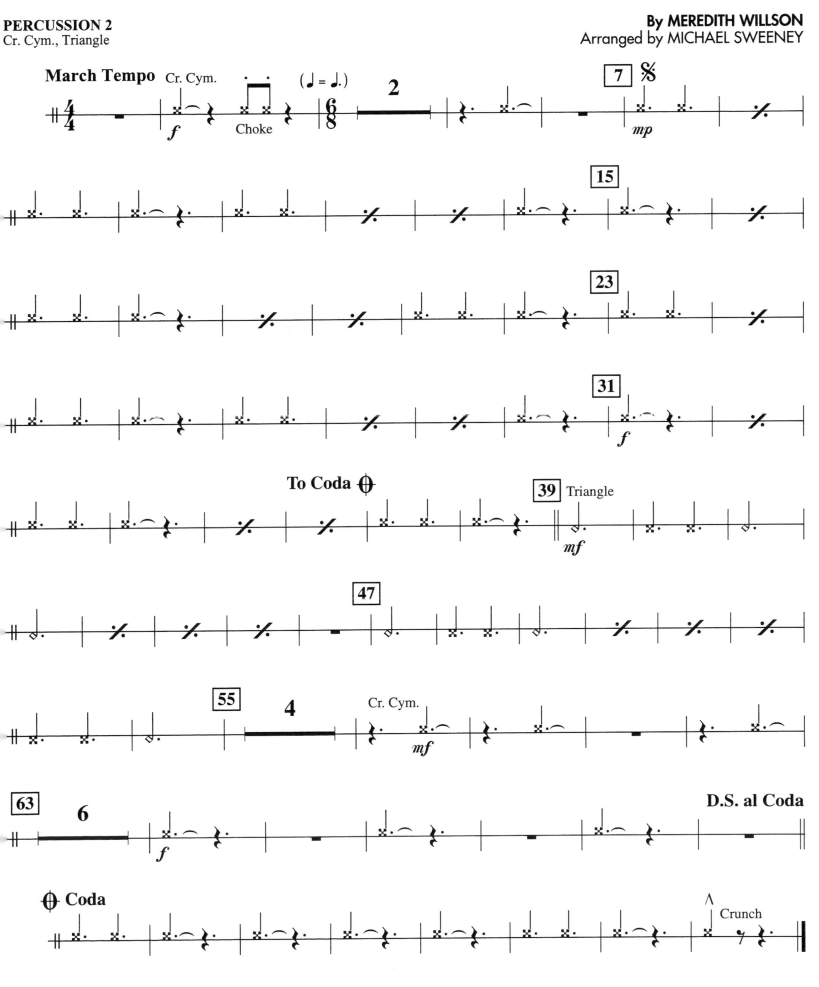